Issue 8411

10 Great Games and How to Use Them

....

Presentation Skills & Games

Editorial Staff for 8411

Editor
Madelyn R. Callahan

Revised 1999

Editor
Cat Sharpe

Contributing Editor
Ann Bruen

Production Design
Anne Morgan

Need a trainer's lifeline? Visit infoline.astd.org.

....

Infoline is a real got-a-problem, find-a-solution publication. Concise and practical, *Infoline* is an information lifeline written specifically for trainers and other workplace learning and performance professionals. Whether the subject is a current trend in the field, or tried-and-true training basics, *Infoline* is a complete, reliable trainer's information resource. *Infoline* is available by subscription and single copy purchase.

Printed in the United States of America.

Selecting and Designing Games

Trainers have long believed in the adage "live and learn." Not surprisingly, they have always known that experience is often the best teacher. Experiential learning in the form of trainer-conducted games is frequently more effective than traditional classroom methods in increasing learning and retention. Research shows that adults learn more effectively by doing—by using their new knowledge and skills—than by passively listening or reading.

One study concluded that within one year, adults are likely to forget 50 percent of what they have learned through exclusively passive methods. Another study indicated that approximately half of one day's learning may be lost during the ensuing 24 hours. In two weeks, an additional 25 percent may be lost.

Games frequently provide the basis for successful training programs. They aid in program preparation, instruction, and evaluation. Their strongest feature is the element of fun that relaxes, motivates, and involves every participant from the outset, making learning enjoyable and productive. Games also use the five basic senses, particularly sight, sound, and touch, making for a more comprehensive and effective learning experience.

Strictly speaking, games are competitive activities governed by rules that define players' actions and determine outcomes. For the purposes of this discussion, we will employ a broad definition of *games* that includes the formalized, competitive activities and various exercises, activities, or demonstrations (also known as structured experiences or participative group exercises).

Other experiential exercises, such as simulation, role play, and simulation games, are addressed in other *Infolines*. These exercises represent a number of either very simple or extremely sophisticated and complex activities. Role play and simulation exercises use real-life situations and applications. Simulation games are both reality based and competitive.

Simple games appeal to a large number of trainers for the following reasons:

■ *Versatility*
Game components can be interchanged easily to create a new focus or an entirely new game, and many different versions of a game can be built on one model.

■ *Cost Effectiveness*
Resource materials for these games are easy to produce and obtain. Some games require no materials at all, and most games involve little more than paper and pencils, which every training budget can afford.

■ *Transfer of Learning*
Learning proceeds from group interaction, with the instructor serving as a guide or resource rather than a detached lecturer or presenter. The instructor facilitates the learning and is an active integral part of the training process.

This issue of *Infoline* will acquaint you with various types of games, their special uses and features, as well as when to use and how to implement them. It will discuss the effective designs and uses of the four most widely used games:

● icebreakers
● competitive games
● exercises
● puzzles

Effective games can have significant impact on your audience. They can sharpen your training session so that your group will comprehend the materials on several levels—cognitive, affective, and empathetic. Such meaningful experiences will increase participation and learning. To accomplish this, be sure to carry out each phase of the game properly and completely.

Start by choosing a room that will accommodate your group comfortably. Check the noise level inside and outside the building. Prepare the seating arrangements in advance, and test acoustics and audiovisual equipment.

Designing Games

Find out as much as you can about your audience, facility, and available resources. Become familiar with a variety of games—their content, time limits, themes, style, format, and required supporting materials. Then decide how you would like to use the game: to identify, examine, critique, or discuss a problem; to develop skills such as empathetic listening, communication, problem solving, decision making, or management; or to start up, conclude, or refresh a program.

Organize your activity by establishing clear and specific objectives. You can proceed on a logical course once you know where you are going. Design resource materials to fit the content, and compile a list of materials for every phase of the game: instruments, forms, information sheets, background reading, diagrams, charts, and props, such as matchsticks, toothpicks, cards, blocks.

Consider the participants' level of interactive training experience to determine how they may respond to particular games. Plan in sequence; each phase of an activity should enhance the next one. Ask another trainer's opinion of your design, and pilot your design by using a test group.

Build into the design ways to gather data: listeners, observers, or questionnaires, for example. Always be certain that games are adaptable to the needs of participants with physical limitations. Determine physical constraints of the game, particularly those that involve movement.

Design Hints

To design games that will enhance your training sessions, follow these tips for success:

- Use a flowchart to plan your steps, and time each step.

- Choose a basic structure—introduction, stages, conclusions—and then add detailed content.

- Prepare all handouts in advance and have them ready.

- Plan for the worst; have back-up activities in case your group is too slow, too quick, or too familiar with your first-choice game.

- Make sure that participants are always actively engaged and challenged.

- Schedule sufficient time for breaks and discussions to alleviate tension.

- Play the game before you use it to make sure you are prepared to administer it properly.

- Be flexible; your game is a learning experience that should evolve naturally.

Conducting Games

Clarify expectations at the beginning of your session and make sure that trainees understand the objectives and game rules. Misunderstanding can lead to resistance and disruptions. Make a contract with the group, agreeing on expectations, roles, responsibilities, and norms. Then make a checklist of participants' expectations; post them and refer to them during the game.

Intervene only when necessary; encourage participants to be assertive and not to rely on you to defend or protect them. Give support and be willing to accept it from the group. Ask for feedback and respond to it (see *Giving and Receiving Feedback* opposite). Be sensitive to whether trainees are comfortable with open or experimental activities. Pick up cues from their behavior and comments. Be prepared to handle participant needs as they arise (see the *The Inevitable Gremlins* on the following page).

Experiment with and learn from your experiences as a facilitator. Maintain good listening skills and a respectful attitude toward trainees by keeping eye contact, repeating for clarity, and answering questions objectively. Be spontaneous and flexible. Whatever the outcome of the game, turn it into a learning experience. Reassure participants that mistakes are part of learning and that they will not be penalized for failures. Finally, close your activities properly by helping participants resolve problems and apply their learning.

The Don'ts of Game Presentation

Guard against these common mistakes made by trainers:

- using excessively difficult or threatening games

- distancing yourself from trainees (share breaks and meals with them)

- using the same techniques repeatedly

- giving long explanations

- changing the game to appease a few people in the group

- becoming more concerned with the game than the learning goals

Facilitating Games

Experts agree that this is the most important step of the learning process. This is the point at which participants examine their experience systematically. Facilitation methods may include a combination of discussion, observer's reports, instrumentation (questionnaires and surveys), and feedback and analysis. Without your planning and guidance, trainees cannot learn adequately. To ensure success, you should do the following things:

- Choose your role in the presentation. Will you act as leader, participant, or observer?

- Decide how trainees will participate: individually, in small groups, or as an entire group?

- Give participants a focus. Should you focus on specific behaviors, attitudes, or problems?

- Decide when to intervene *during* the activity in addition to providing wrap-up procedures.

- Provide supplies such as paper, pencils, markers, flipcharts, forms, and graphs.

Giving and Receiving Feedback

Games, like any learning situation, benefit greatly from constructive feedback. The following considerations will help you improve your group's productivity and participation:

- Establish a climate for testing new behaviors, taking risks, sharing information, and exploring alternatives.

- Establish feedback norms for listening, asking questions, and describing behaviors.

- Listen to and try to understand others' points of view without personal bias.

- Ask questions to get a thorough understanding of the problem. Show your interest with open-ended questions that invite comprehensive rather than yes-or-no answers.

- Be specific. Focus feedback on participants' behavior rather than on their qualities.

- Focus feedback on observations rather than inferences, on what you can see or hear rather than interpretations and conclusions. If you share interpretations and conclusions (it is sometimes valuable to do this), identify them as such.

- Describe the particular behaviors exhibited *during the game*. Do not be concerned with general or known behaviors associated with group members.

- Specify strengths first, then offer concrete suggestions for improving other areas. For example, say, "You are very articulate and observant, but you are most effective when you focus directly on particular discussion themes."

- Ask for a reaction to your suggestion. The trainee may not accept or may want to modify your suggestion.

- Try to close your discussions with agreements, particularly during the processing of competitive games. If you have listened to one another and clarified your ideas, you should be able to agree on specific changes and plans for improvement.

The Inevitable Gremlins

Every trainer must confront the dreaded gremlins of training sessions: the clowns, the hecklers, the disagreeable know-it-alls who manage to disrupt at least 10 minutes of your presentation. If it has not happened already, it is bound to sooner than you think. Take a look at the following pointers; they may make your life easier some day.

- Listen to the disruptive participants and let them know you are interested in their opinions.

- Give them responsibilities by asking them to be observers and to record others' viewpoints. Disruptive behavior is often an attempt to be heard; tell your dissidents that you welcome their *positive* contributions.

- Ask questions to find out what the problem participant really feels and needs.

- If personal problems cause the behavior, speak to the participant privately. Disrupters may become more cooperative once they have talked through problems.

- Reward cooperation and serious contributions.

- Never argue. Restate hostile questions in mild language and direct your answers to the group rather than the heckler. Remain calm and patient. If you lose your temper, your audience may decide to support the heckler.

- Rephrase superficial or hostile questions as statements so that the questioner must take a position.

- Form groups of two to five participants so the disrupter will no longer influence the entire group.

- Use processing time to discuss the activity or program in progress and to emphasize expectations and norms. The discussion will undoubtedly include the problem of disruptive behavior.

- Turn the disrupter over to the group. If a participant wants to argue with you, ask for responses from the group.

- Tell persistent arguers that you would like to hear more of their opinions during a break or after the exercise.

- Ask the disrupter to compare theirs and other members' ideas and to restate others' ideas. This will force the disrupter to listen to and understand other perspectives.

- Compliment the opinions of your talkative participants, but make it a point to solicit the input of less vocal members.

- Deal with class clowns by asking them to explain their remarks in objective terms so that everyone can comprehend their statements.

- Control sidetracking by asking the disrupter and the group to relate off-subject comments to discussion themes.

Facilitating Hints

There are a number of guidelines that are specific to facilitating games. Assess actual learning and determine the degree of goal accomplishment; then examine the reasons for similarities and differences in these two areas. Share discoveries about the learning process as well as personal discoveries, and analyze impressions of how the group worked together. Identify strengths and areas for improvement.

Decide how to apply the training to jobs. Examine personal and job-related changes and make specific plans to implement the changes. Finally, suggest ways to improve the game.

Icebreakers

Whatever the facilitator does at the beginning of a presentation sets the tone for the rest of the training. Thus there is a need for some sort of activity that will get your participants warmed up—an icebreaker.

Icebreakers present program materials in a more interesting way than introductory lectures by instantly involving the entire group; participants become acquainted by sharing personal attitudes, values, and concerns. Nonthreatening activities relax participants and reduce anxiety, encouraging spontaneity even among timid and shy trainees.

Icebreakers establish the pace and tone of the program and help build enthusiasm. They motivate the group quickly with activities that involve physical and emotional energy. In addition, they orient participants to the group's resources and give the group a sense of identity, helping to build trust. Finally, they establish the identity of the trainer as a facilitator rather than a lecturer. For examples of icebreakers, see *What's My Line* at right and *Roles of a Good Trainee* on the next page.

Icebreakers acquaint participants with one another and put them at ease (trainees are more receptive when they are ready to learn). These nonthreatening warm-up activities make a smooth start by introducing and focusing the program. They let participants know that *they* are responsible for their learning and that the trainer's job is to facilitate the learning. They also show participants what kind of trainer you are—demonstrative or reserved, conventional or innovative, program or participant oriented.

15 Icebreaker Tips

To properly set the stage for your training program, follow these icebreaker guidelines:

1. Develop an environment conducive to group interaction by providing a common experience or helping the group share experiences.

2. Never *insist* that participants share personal data.

3. If a trainee is using too much time during a personal statement, intervene tactfully and put the group back on course.

4. Determine the length of your opening activities by estimating the duration of the program (a four-hour session would require only six or seven minutes of icebreakers).

5. Consider your group's expectations when determining the level of activity and involvement of your icebreakers.

What's My Line?

Objective

To illustrate the importance of first impressions and stereotyping.

Procedure

This is a variation of the self-introduction game, using name, job, and favorite hobby. Instead of introducing themselves, however, participants are asked to introduce the person on their right, using strictly guesswork—that is, no clues are exchanged.

After a brief observation of the person on their right, ask participants to introduce him or her with a first name, job, and favorite hobby that they "think" he or she has, giving brief reasons for their guesses.

The person being guessed will then respond with the correct information before proceeding with his or her own introduction. Continue around the circle until everyone has been introduced. (If participants have done the first part of this exercise in a small group, have them return to a large group setting, positioning themselves so that the same person is still on their right. Participants will then introduce the person on their right to the larger group.)

Discussion Questions

1. How accurate are first impressions? What do we base them on?

2. Have you ever opted not to meet someone, based on your first impressions?

3. What are stereotypes? Why do we make them?

4. Do you now feel more comfortable with this group than when you arrived?

5. Do you know more about the people here than when you first arrived?

Materials Required

None.

Approximate Time Required

20–30 minutes.

Jacqueline V. Markus, Department of Communication, Arizona State University, Tempe, AZ

Roles of a Good Trainee

Objective

To create a constructive climate for discussion in a training session.

Procedure

In many groups of entry-level trainees, the participants have previously attended few, if any, formal training programs. Therefore, it is often helpful to establish clear norms for what constitutes acceptable (productive) trainee behavior.

One way to accomplish this quickly, with a certainty of hitting the "right" rules, is to present (orally, by handout, or by overhead transparency) a set of predeveloped guidelines for behaviors that trainees would ideally engage in or avoid. This approach has the advantage of clarity, but has the potential danger of creating a limiting, rule-filled environment. Presented in a positive manner, however, with the use of a handout such as the following example (especially when it is "spiced up" with some humorous illustrations), this exercise can have considerable success.

Example:

Roles of a Trainer (Facilitator)

1. Challenges thinking.

2. Creates lists.

3. Summarizes.

4. Shares ideas.

5. Provides handouts.

6. Serves as a model.

7. Raises questions.

8. Guides discussion.

9. Restates ideas.

10. Provides constructive criticism.

Alternative Procedures

1. Engage the group (early in the session) in a discussion of the productive and nonproductive behaviors they have seen (or can think of) on the part of seminar participants. This has the value of involving them in the creation of their own norms for their behavior.

2. Prepare printed tent cards with participants' names on the front and five rules of appropriate seminar behavior on the back. While the name faces outward to the trainer and other trainees, the rules are visually present to the trainee at all times as a constant reminder.

Materials Required

Possible handout, transparency, or tent cards.

Approximate Time Required

5–10 minutes.

From Games Trainers Play, *by E.E. Scannell and J.W. Newstrom. Copyright 1980 by McGraw-Hill Book Company, New York. Used with permission. All rights reserved.*

6. Select activities that will be appealing to specific kinds of groups. For instance, machine operators might not be as receptive to activities involving fantasies or imagination as would therapists.

7. Consider the background of your group and temper innovative activities with the knowledge of their cultural preferences.

8. Choose opening activities that are appropriate for the particular program. Employee motivation programs, for example, may use more flexible activities than management development programs.

9. Use icebreakers that involve physical energy to stimulate your group.

10. Use icebreakers as an opportunity for *you* to become acquainted with your group.

11. Use them to indicate what will be expected of the group and what the group can expect of the program.

12. Use them to show how you intend to participate in the program.

13. Choose icebreakers that will establish an environment for discussion.

14. Use icebreakers you are comfortable with. Some experiential activities may take time and participants' attention away from the specific subject matter. If you prefer more conventional methods that give you more control, use them.

15. Avoid using icebreakers for very large groups in which they will lose their intensity.

Competitive Games

Turning games into competitions helps to break up the routine of your training session. Participants can have fun and learn at the same time.

Competitive games are active, experiential forms of learning; that is, participants learn from their own actions rather than from what others tell them. This active involvement is motivational—most trainees respond to competition and the incentive to win. In addition, games appeal to learners of differing abilities, because everyone has the opportunity for involvement, and the valuable experience gained from games makes everyone a winner. Moreover, games provide a safe atmosphere for taking risks, away from real-world penalties for mistakes.

Games help trainees retain information and encourage unself-conscious behavior that can be analyzed in discussions. Games are social as well as educational tools, providing participants information about their own behavior in relation to others. For examples of competitive games, see *The Number Game* and *Archeological Game* on the following pages.

Games energize participants and promote interaction. They engage participants' interest and attention and provide them with a common experience. Games reinforce learning and training by demonstration. Among the skills they develop are strategic and critical thinking, communication, negotiation, problem solving, and decision making. Competitive games can inject energy into a low point of the program after lunch or at the end of the day, or they can be used to recap important points and close a presentation.

15 Competitive Game Tips

To use competitive games to best advantage, follow these guidelines:

1. Keep games in line with learning objectives.

2. Be familiar with your game. Trainees cannot be enthusiastic if they are interrupted constantly with corrections of game instructions.

3. Prepare by playing the game several times with friends.

The Number Game

Objective

To allow participants to discover (or reinforce) some principles of adult learning through hands-on activity.

Procedure

Distribute eight copies of "The Number Game" to each participant. Ask them to place a blank sheet of paper over the numbers so they cannot see the placement of the numbers. Tell them this is a simple hand-eye coordination exercise in which they are to work as fast as they can within a given time period. Then tell the participants: "Remove the blank sheet of paper. With pen or pencil, draw a line from No. 1 to No. 2, to No. 3, and so forth, until I say 'Stop.' OK? Go!"

Allow 60 seconds, and then say: "Stop. Please circle the highest number you reached and jot down the number '1' in the upper right-hand corner."

Repeat this procedure seven more times, each time allowing 60 seconds. Make sure each sheet is numbered in sequence.

Discussion Questions

1. In all candor, how did you feel when you were going through the exercise? (*Note:* Responses will be "nervous," "frustrated," "upset," "mad," and so forth.)

2. "Practice makes perfect." If this is really true, we all should have shown a consistent increase in the number attained with each attempt. Is that true for each of you? If not, why?

3. Did anyone have an increase every time?

4. Many of us experienced a slight decline, or "learning plateau." What might cause this?

5. If our trainees are likely to experience these plateaus, how can we be more understanding of these situations and adapt to them?

Materials Required

A quantity of "The Number Game" sheets (4 per person, printed on both sides).

Approximate Time Required

15 minutes.

From Games Trainers Play, *by E.E. Scannell and J.W. Newstrom. Copyright 1980 by McGraw-Hill Book Company, New York. Used with permission. All rights reserved.*

Archeological Game

Objective

To point up how our screening mechanism filters out unwanted data, details, minutiae. This is important so we can get through the day and get our tasks accomplished without being sidetracked by trivia bombardment.

Note: This objective is *not* given to participants, since this perceptual phenomenon is what they will learn from the game.

Procedure

Give the participants the following instructions:

1. "You are to function as archeologists. This means you are interested in reconstructing a given culture based on artifacts you discover.

2. The culture you are concerned with is the United States in the year 7000.

3. You are in a 'dig' and come up with a small, flat, round object. It has a man's face on it; the man has a beard. The object is a U.S. penny and has this year's date on it.

4. *Without* reaching for a penny from your pocket or purse, come up with as many characteristics of the U.S. coin and culture at that date as you can. This is what archeologists do all the time. You will have to rely on your memory to recall the data on the penny. You are in competition with the other teams. You have five minutes for the task."

At the five-minute mark, call time and ask participants to total their cultural characteristics. (The totals typically run in the "teens.") Get a verbal report from the team with the highest number of characteristics, and list its data on a flipchart. Anticipate items such as these:

- bilingual (English and Latin)
- architecture (if Lincoln Memorial is on rear)
- system of writing
- appearance conscious (Lincoln's beard)
- liberty loving (liberty)
- metallurgy
- calendar
- coinage system

- hero worship (Lincoln)
- a federal government ("E Pluribus Unum")
- religion ("In God We Trust")
- mining
- sewing skills or tailoring (Lincoln's shirt and coat)
- cloth production
- dress conscious (coat, tie)
- system of numbers
- agriculture (if a "wheat" penny)
- patriarchal society

Also anticipate friendly rivalry—the losing team will deny the validity of certain cultural traits listed by the winning team. Add (new) items from the other teams to your flipchart list.

Discussion

To process the game, ask participants what was learned. Some possible responses from the groups (list on a flipchart) are: importance of teamwork (several heads are better than one); a group leader is not necessary; importance of background or perception (different groups see different things).

At this point, add: "I'd like to pick up on the perception aspect. Was the task difficult to do, relying solely on memory?" [Participants respond "Yes."] "Why was it difficult to remember what is on an object that you handle *daily?*" [Pause at this point, for this is *the* profound question of the game.] Some possible participant answers are: "We don't pay attention to it. It's not important information. We take it for granted."

At this point, say: "Yes, we overlook the detail, the trivia, because we have a mechanism in our heads (phenomenon of perceptual choice or selective attention) that screens out the unimportant. This is a tremendously helpful device because it allows us to get through the day without getting bogged down by the innumerable stimuli that bombard us constantly—trees, signs, houses, stores, cars, clothing, colors. But at the same time, our screening mechanism may work the other way. It may screen out data we *should be cognizant of*—for example, to call old Harry to our meeting. We forget him, and he gets mad at us. So our screening device works for good and for less than good. We must be aware of this perceptual process and try to keep it from overlooking the important stimuli, which also are out there."

From The Winning Trainer *by J.E. Eitington.*
Copyright 1984 by Gulf Publishing, Houston, TX. Used with permission. All rights reserved.

4. Organize all game materials and keep extra supplies of paper, pencils, and other items that are used up quickly or are easily misplaced.

5. If you are using handouts, know when to distribute them for greatest impact and least disruption.

6. Choose comfortable and workable seating and space arrangements.

7. Play the game at the time when participants will benefit most—during the introduction, instruction, or conclusion of your program.

8. Do not over-explain the game; introduce it briefly. If you use a written statement, make sure it is clear and precise.

9. Take questions only after you have completed your explanation. This will also give you time to ease into the game.

10. Choose a method of forming groups that best suits your particular game. If your objective is to build trust, random selection would produce groups of unacquainted individuals. Groups of two or three are ideal for sharing personal data. Groups of people who are wearing one or more of the same colors may also agree on other topics and work well as a team.

11. Refrain from intervening in the game frequently. Participants are playing the game to learn from their interaction with one another.

12. Avoid the role of trainer as authority figure or expert.

13. Assess learning and outcomes without appearing as a strict "evaluator."

14. Remind participants of the time five to 10 minutes before the game is scheduled to end.

15. Allow sufficient time for the entire activity when you plan your program schedule. Games that must be continued later lose momentum, and participants may lose interest before the outcomes.

Exercises

Exercises are structured learning experiences that help to enhance the training atmosphere. They are versatile instruments that can be used in a variety of ways.

Exercises accommodate a wide range of formats and purposes—short or long, simple or complex. They are conducted by the trainer, the group, or both. Exercises can be oriented either toward individuals or groups (of any size). Some exercises involve physical movement while others focus on discussion or writing, but they do not all require supporting materials. They can be made into games by adding competition.

Numerous sources for exercises exist—publishers, colleagues, or training programs—but they also can be created by trainers to suit specific needs, or they can use input from the group members themselves or from supervisors. For examples of exercises, see *Hand to Chin Exercise, One- and Two-Way Communication, What Do People Want from Their Jobs?* and *The Lemon Exchange*.

Exercises can be used to open or close a presentation, to illustrate specific learning goals, or to reinforce learning. They put participants at ease and maintain high participant involvement. In addition, exercises generate information for analyzing a particular problem or behavior and facilitate general and personal learning.

16 Exercise Tips

To make sure that you use exercises to their fullest advantage, follow these guidelines:

1. Select exercises that will fulfill your learning objectives best. Then consider the element of fun.

2. Organize all resource materials and equipment in advance.

3. Make sure the group understands instructions. Hand out written instructions if necessary.

4. Be straightforward.

5. Use relevant practical content that trainees can apply to their personal or job-related goals.

6. Use realistic time frames.

7. Choose the most effective time during the program to use your exercise. If you use it too early in the program, participants may miss the point; too late, and they may be less attentive.

8. Avoid covering too much material. If participants appear overwhelmed, edit extraneous material without causing breaks or long pauses in the activity.

9. Determine when to intervene *during* the exercise, particularly for the longer, more complex exercises.

10. Remind the group of the learning objectives throughout the activity.

11. Clarify your role in the learning process so trainees will know how you can assist them.

12. Show trainees that you identify with the group and are interested in learning with them. Sometimes this may include participating in the exercise.

13. If the exercise is long and multifaceted, use a summary sheet to help reinforce the training.

14. Use facilitation procedures that are appropriate for your group.

15. If you use observers, prepare them adequately with background information.

16. Avoid serious conflicts, too much emphasis on fun, or the generation of too much data. These problems will inhibit discussion and facilitation.

Hand to Chin Exercise

Objective

To illustrate that actions may speak louder than words.

Procedure

As you demonstrate, ask the group to extend their right arms parallel to the floor. Say, "Now, make a circle with your thumb and forefinger." [Demonstrate the action as you speak.] Then continue, "Now, very firmly bring your hand to your chin." [*Note:* As you say, "Bring your hand to your chin," bring your hand to your *cheek,* not your chin.] Pause. [Most of the group will have done what you have, that is, brought their hands to their cheeks.] Look around, but say nothing. After 5–10 seconds, a few in the group will realize their error and move their hands to their chins. After a few more seconds, more people will join in the laughter, and your point can then be verbally reinforced—a trainer's actions may speak louder than words.

Discussion Questions

1. Did you ever hear the saying, "Don't do as I do; do as I say"? Do we practice this as trainers?

2. We all know actions speak louder than words. How can we use this knowledge in our jobs to help ensure better understanding?

3. Communication is always a scapegoat for performance problems. What other barriers to effective communication does this exercise suggest?

Materials Required

None.

Approximate Time Required

5 minutes.

From Games Trainers Play, *by E.E. Scannell and J.W. Newstrom. Copyright 1980 by McGraw-Hill Book Company, New York. Used with permission. All rights reserved.*

One- and Two-Way Communication

Objective

To demonstrate the many problems of misunderstanding that can occur in a one-way communication.

Procedure

Prepare a diagram similar to the one shown here. Ask a volunteer to assist in this demonstration. Explain to the group that the volunteer is going to describe something to them, and their task is to simply follow instructions in sketching out the illustration.

Give the volunteer the figure. Have the volunteer turn his or her back to the audience so no eye contact is possible. The volunteer can use only verbal communication (no gestures, hand signals). Furthermore, no questions are allowed on the part of the group. In brief, only one-way communication is allowed. When the exercise is completed, project the correct figure on the overhead projector and ask participants to judge whether their drawings are at all similar to it.

Discussion Questions

1. How many of us got confused and just quit listening? Why?

2. Why was the one-way communication so difficult to follow?

3. Even two-way communication cannot ensure complete understanding. How can we make our communication efforts more effective?

One-Way Communication Diagram

(*Note:* If time permits, this activity can be immediately followed with another volunteer using a comparable illustration but allowing for full and free two-way communication.)

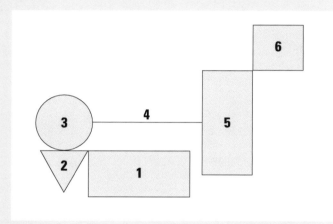

Materials Required

Diagram, as shown.

Approximate Time Required

10–20 minutes.

From Games Trainers Play, *by E.E. Scannell and J.W. Newstrom. Copyright 1980 by McGraw-Hill, New York. Used with permission. All rights reserved.*

What Do People Want from Their Jobs?

Objective

To give participants an opportunity to discuss what factors motivate employees.

Procedure

Distribute copies of the form, "What Do People Want from Their Jobs?" Divide the group into subgroups of three to five people each. Ask each person to indicate which of the 10 items listed is thought to be of *most* importance in contributing to employee morale. Weight the items from 1 through 10, assigning 10 to the most important item, 9 for the next, and so forth, in a reverse order so that all 10 numbers are used.

Have each group total the individual weights within their group. Rank the 10 items under the column marked "Group."

Advise the group that this same scale has been given to thousands of workers around the country. In comparing rankings of both employees and supervisors, the typical supervisory group is ranked in the order shown under "Factors."

When employees are given the same exercise, however, and asked what affects their morale the most, their answers tend to follow this pattern [mark in the "Employees" column]:

1. Full appreciation of work done

2. Feeling of being in on things

3. Help on personal problems

4. Job security

5. High wages

6. Interesting work

7. Promotion in the company

8. Personal loyalty of supervisor

9. Good working conditions

10. Tactful discipline

Note that the top three items marked by the employees are the last three thought to be important for them by their supervisors.

Discussion Questions

1. In comparing your group's ratings with those of other groups ("Employees" column), what factors might account for differences of opinion?

2. Why might supervisory evaluations ("Supervisors" column) be so different from their employees ("Employees" column)?

3. If this form were to be used in your department or office, how similar would the results be?

Materials Required

Copies of the form "What Do People Want from Their Jobs?"

Approximate Time Required

20 minutes.

What Do People Want from Their Jobs?

Individual	Group	Factors	Supervisors	Employees
		High Wages		
		Job Security		
		Promotion in the Company		
		Good Working Conditions		
		Interesting Work		
		Personal Loyalty of Supervisor		
		Tactful Discipline		
		Full Appreciation of Work Done		
		Help on Personal Problems		
		Feeling of Being in on Things		

From Games Trainers Play, *by E.E. Scannell and J.W. Newstrom. Copyright 1980 by McGraw-Hill, New York. Used with permission. All rights reserved.*

The Lemon Exchange

Objective

To vividly illustrate the importance of individual differences, the need for astute observational skills, and sensitivity to personal characteristics.

Procedure

Bring an adequate supply of lemons (or almost any fruit).

1. Distribute one to each member of the group. Direct each person to examine his or her lemon carefully by rolling it, squeezing it, and so forth. Ask them to *get to know their lemon* (always good for a few laughs). Tell them to pick a name for it. Encourage them to identify in their minds the strengths and weaknesses of their lemon.

2. Collect all the lemons and mix them up in front of the group.

3. Spread out all the lemons on a table and ask participants to come forward and select their original lemon. If conflicts develop over their choices, assist the parties in reconciling their differences, or simply note the failure to agree and use that as a basis for later discussion. (*Note:* In smaller groups of up to 25 people, the vast majority successfully identify their own lemons.)

Discussion Questions

1. How many are very sure they reclaimed their original lemon? How do you know?

2. What parallels are there between differentiating many lemons and differentiating many people? What differences are there?

3. Why can't we get to know people just as rapidly as we did our lemons? What role does the skin play (for lemons and for people)?

4. What human behavior does this bring to light?

Materials Required

A sufficient quantity of lemons (or other appropriate substitute).

Approximate Time Required

20–30 minutes.

From Games Trainers Play, *by E.E. Scannell and J.W. Newstrom. Copyright 1980 by McGraw-Hill, New York. Used with permission. All rights reserved.*

Puzzles

Puzzles are another valuable means of enhancing your learning environment. Like icebreakers, competitive games, and exercises, they encourage active participation.

Puzzles are versatile in form and use, and can be used as either solo or group games. They can be solved orally; visually—with handouts, charts, or blackboards; or physically—with blocks, straws, or sticks. Puzzles are more comfortable ways of exploring ability than stressful, inhibiting exams. They encourage imaginative solutions to problems without the pressure to "be creative." By illustrating alternatives, puzzles point out the value of investigating possibilities in areas such as career planning, taking risks, and assessing the potential of others.

Puzzles illustrate that effective approaches to problem solving use personal touch as well as logical thought. Participants can see themselves improve as they become better at solving the puzzles. This builds confidence and helps develop skills for planning strategies. Puzzles also let people know how they compare with others. For an example, see *Cake Cutting Puzzle,* opposite.

Puzzles involve everyone in an activity and engage the participants' curiosity and imagination. By providing variety and novelty, they show that learning can be exciting and interesting. Puzzles reinforce learning by explaining subject matter or by introducing and demonstrating the importance of both creative and logical approaches to problem solving. They also can be used to break the ice and put participants at ease.

12 Puzzle Tips

To use puzzles effectively, follow these guidelines:

1. De-emphasize the idea that "brain teasers," word games, crossword puzzles, and other puzzles require superior cognitive skills. Less confident participants may avoid puzzles that reveal shortcomings.

2. Use moderately difficult puzzles to stimulate your audience. Extremely difficult puzzles will frustrate and alienate trainees.

Cake Cutting Puzzle

Procedure

Draw an aerial view of a cake on the flipchart as shown in figure 1. Tell the group: "A woman had baked a cake for her party to be attended by eight guests. Her (and your) task is to produce eight pieces of cake with only three cuts of the knife."

Figure 1. Can you produce eight pieces of cake with only three cuts of the knife?

Bird's eye view

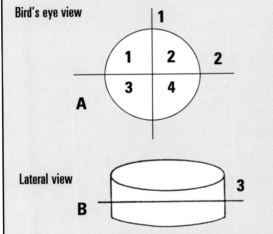

Lateral view

Figure 2. Lateral Cut Method: (A) Right angle intersecting cuts produce four pieces; (B) a lateral cut produces eight pieces.

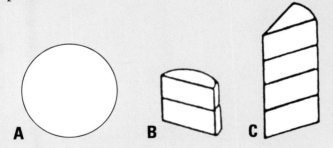

Figure 3. Stacking Method: (A) A vertical cut down the middle produces two pieces; (B) stacking the two pieces and cutting them vertically produces four pieces; (C) a final stacking and cutting of the pieces produces eight pieces.

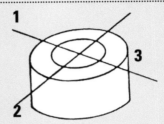

Figure 4. Center Cut Method: Two vertical cuts and then a center circular cut are made to produce eight pieces.

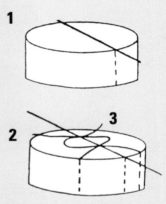

Figure 5. Disgustingly Sneaky Method: Two curved lines and a center straight cut produce eight unequal pieces.

Note: No one said the pieces had to be equal or the cuts made via a straight line. Remember, this is her party with her guests, and she can cut the cake any way she wishes.

Discussion

Ask: "What does the puzzle tell us?" Some answers are: "There may be more options than we think; let's stretch our imaginations and we can produce solutions that are varied and unique."

The puzzle may be used to stimulate thinking about problem solving, creating approaches, and alternative seeking.

3. Choose a straightforward puzzle. Some puzzles distance the activity from its purpose.

4. Explain objectives clearly and succinctly at the beginning so that these can be reinforced throughout the activity and the entire training program.

5. Always have a back-up puzzle in case too many trainees are familiar with your first choice.

6. Encourage trainees to approach the puzzles with the intention of taking risks and exceeding their self-imposed limitations.

7. Select a puzzle with a variety of solutions so that the activity is open to creative approaches.

8. Challenge your trainees to find new approaches and options.

9. Make them aware of the valuable uses of right-brain, creative thinking, but point out that there are times when logical left-brain thinking is more appropriate.

10. Keep a large stock of supplies. Participants often make several attempts and many mistakes before they solve puzzles.

11. Always budget enough time to integrate the experience into the training. Most puzzles are representative and must be interpreted at the conclusion.

12. Use puzzles simply for fun, as a change of pace, or to relax or stimulate participants. Puzzles offer a refreshing break from learning, enabling participants to resume their training with renewed energy.

Playing Those Mind Games

Researcher David Meier conducted a study that focused on the use of *mental imagery*—"the guided, self-controlled or spontaneous imagining of any thing or situation that can be seen, touched, smelled, heard, tasted, or experienced in any way." Through his research, he concluded that learning tools using fantasy and the imagination improve retention and recall.

Meier also described a mental imagery training technique, known as *guided imagery*, by which trainers use mental imagery to help trainees do the following:

- develop management skills

- set goals

- reduce stress

- increase confidence and assertiveness

- improve memory, communication, and problem-solving skills

- augment conventional training

These techniques provide experiential activities that are guided by a facilitator and carried out with a partner or by the entire group. For an example of how to use mental imagery, see Meier's professional development game opposite.

Development Through Mental Imagery

This game can be played with groups of any size. Its purpose is to help people identify their unique talents and strengths and discover how best to use them in their professional lives. The group leader can use the following script as a guide, varying it with experience to fit the needs of each specific group. The total time for this procedure is approximately 45 minutes.

■ Introduction

In just 45 minutes you will have a better understanding of what your unique talents and strengths are, and you will have a wealth of ideas of how best to use them to achieve higher levels of professional success and satisfaction. You will gain insight and a positive new sense of direction in your career. And you will come out of this experience with a set of guidelines for developing and enriching your professional life over the next year or so. This insight and direction will not come from me, but from you. I will provide the form, but you will provide 100 percent of the content. You will probably find the form to be fun. We will use mental imagery followed by reflection and analysis. In the first imagery session, we will ask you to vividly review in your mind three peak experiences of your life and to become aware of the unique strengths and talents you exhibited in those experiences. Then, after analysis, we will ask you to step into the future and see yourself exhibiting those strengths and talents flawlessly and effortlessly in your professional life. We will ask you to observe what you are doing, and from that, to design your own marching orders for peak performance over the next year.

(*Note:* In the script that follows, the virgule (/) indicates a pause. Most pauses can be for three to five seconds, but follow your intuition when you are in the situation.)

■ Preparation

To prepare for the first imagery experience, just get comfortable and relaxed. You can do this easily by breathing a bit more deeply than usual and becoming aware of your breath/ just concentrate on your breath/ just let your whole attention focus on the feeling of the air coming into your body/ notice how pleasurable it is to breathe/ concentrate on the pleasure of breathing/ as you breathe in, feel your whole body being refreshed/ a tingling sensation/ energy/ and each time you exhale, let go/ relax/ inhale and receive pleasure and new energy/ exhale and relax/ becoming more filled with quiet energy/ becoming more deeply relaxed with every breath/ continue doing this for a moment, closing your eyes and getting ready to enter the rich world of your deep inner mind.

■ First Imagery Session (five minutes)

Return in your imagination now to a peak experience of your life. Relive a time when your unique strengths and talents shone without obstruction—a time when you were filled with energy and an easy flowing personal power—a time when you were free, open, fulfilled, fully alive, fully

yourself in all your strength/ relive this situation now/ how old are you?/ where are you?/ what are you doing, saying, feeling?/ be totally back there now/ and observe what strengths you are manifesting and how this feels/ take a moment to relive this experience fully now, with total recall and total awareness/// (pause for about one minute).

Now move away from this scene and pick a second time and place in your past that was a peak experience—a time when you were filled with energy and an easy flowing personal power/ (continue as above).

Now move away from this scene and pick a third and final time and place in your life that was a peak experience for you—a time when you were filled with energy and an easy flowing personal power/ (continue as above).

■ Analysis

We will bring the imagery session to a close now and ask that when you are ready, you return to this time and place, open your eyes gradually, and get ready to reflect on the experiences you have just had.

Divide a piece of paper sideways into three columns. In each column, record your deepest impressions of each of your three imagery experiences. Use words, pictures, or a combination of both. Just capture in any way you can some of the most important elements of each experience. Reflect particularly on what each experience has to teach you about your unique talents and strengths. Work quickly and without criticism. We will allow three or four minutes for this.

Now debrief with a partner. Find a partner and share your experience and insight at any level you care to. Most important, help each other find the common thread that runs through your three peak experiences. Help each other determine what all three experiences are saying about your unique talents and strengths. We will take about five minutes for this.

Now by yourself, spend the next two minutes synthesizing everything you have experienced thus far down into its essence. Create an annotated list of what you now perceive to be your main unique strengths and talents.

■ Second Imagery Session (five minutes)

You have now identified your unique talents and strengths. We want you to enter the world of your imagination a second time now to experience what it is like to manifest these talents and strengths fully in your professional life over the next year or so. You will enter the future and actually experience yourself exercising these talents and strengths in new and creative ways in your professional life. Out of this experience will come some rich and valuable insights regarding how you can direct your professional life for the maximum benefit both to you and to the organization and people you serve.

Your deeper mind already knows what you can do and must do to fully manifest your unique strengths and talents in your professional life. Through an imagery experience, you will now discover what that is.

Let's begin by becoming comfortable and deeply relaxed. (Repeat the instructions of the initial preparation session above.)

Now just let yourself become aware of the needs, problems, and opportunities that exist in your organization or your profession for which your unique talents and strengths are a good fit. Project yourself forward now to a situation where you have successfully met one of these needs, problems, or opportunities in a creative and exceptional way. You have shone. You have that feeling of success and fulfillment and deep satisfaction. You have been able to bring some of your unique talent and strength to bear, and it has worked beautifully. Be in that situation now/ feel how good it is to exercise your unique talents fully, to be fully alive, confident, successful, satisfied/ imagine yourself in that situation now/ what does it feel like?/ what do you see and hear around you?/ what is it that you have done?/ how have you done it?/ what were the steps that led up to your high performance, your success?/ see it all very vividly now/ and take a minute or so to observe everything you can about this situation in great detail/// (pause for about one minute).

Move away from this scene now and enter another one that speaks to another need, problem, or opportunity. Create a second situation, experiencing it even more deeply and vividly, where you have successfully exercised your unique strength and talent in your professional life. You have just turned in a truly exceptional performance/ feel the pride and the quiet satisfaction/ where are you now?/ what do you see and hear and feel?/ what, specifically, were you so successful at?/ what did you do?/ how did that come about?/ what were the specific steps that led up to your success and your sense of full satisfaction that you have now?/ experience this fully for a minute or so and observe everything with total awareness/// (pause for about one minute).

■ *Analysis*

We will bring the imagery session to a close now and ask that when you are ready, you return to this time and place, open your eyes gradually, and get ready to reflect on the experiences you have just had.

Now write nonstop for four minutes about your experience. What did you do? How did you do it? What were the steps that led up to your success? What allowed your talents and strengths to be fully exercised? What product, services, or benefits resulted from what you did? Write first on your first episode. Use words, pictures, anything to capture the essence of that experience. I will stop you in two minutes and ask you to go on to your second episode/// (pause for two minutes).

Now go on to your second episode, capturing in words and pictures as quickly as you can the essence of that experience. What strength and talent did you exercise? How did this manifest itself? What did you do and how did you do it? Write nonstop for two minutes/// (pause for two minutes).

Now debrief with your partner for five minutes, each of you sharing your experience at any level you care to.

(*Note:* At this point, distribute a handout to the participants that is a blank piece of paper with the following written on top: **Specific things I will do in the next year to exercise my talents to the fullest and be exceptionally successful and fulfilled in my work.**)

For the final exercise, complete this handout in any way that is most meaningful and useful to you. Be specific. What do you plan to do? How do you plan to do it? Mention specific people, places, dates, products, services, outcomes—whatever is most appropriate to your situation. You will be creating your job description, your marching orders, your professional development plan, for the next year or so. Be as detailed as you can, and use additional paper if you need it. We will take about 10 minutes to complete this final exercise.

■ *Close*

(*Note:* There are a number of options for closing this session, depending on the nature of the group and the amount of time remaining. Participants could have a final five-minute debriefing with a partner—preferably a different one than they had been working with. Or participants could share their main goals with the entire group for further feedback, suggestions, and refinement.)

Then, with a sense of how your unique strengths can be used to best advantage, go out and do it.

Contributed by David Meier

References & Resources

Articles

Abbott, Katherine. "Games That Work with Techies." *Inside Technology Training*, September 1998, p. 24.

Berry, Bart A. "Getting Training Started on the Right Foot." *Training & Development,* February 1994, pp. 19-22.

Boyd, Susan. "Ten Ways to Break the Ice Before and During Class." *Technical Training,* May/June 1998, pp. 6-7.

Duffy, Joseph R. "Creative Management: Does It Work?" *Quality Digest,* July 1991, pp. 58-67.

Ensher, Ellen A., and Jeanne Hartley. "The Employee Relations Game." *Training & Development,* December 1992, pp. 21-23.

Gunsch, Dawn. "Games Augment Diversity Training." *Personnel Journal,* June 1993, pp. 78-83.

Ireland, Karin. "The Ethics Game." *Personnel Journal,* March 1991, pp. 72-75.

Kirk, James J. "Playing Games Productively." *Training & Development,* August 1997, pp. 11-12.

Mattimore, Bryan W. "Imagine That!" *Training & Development,* July 1994, pp. 28-32.

McIlvaine, Andrew R. "Work Ethics." *Human Resource Executive,* August 1998, pp. 30-34.

Phoon, Annie. "Memory Massage: Review Games That Enhance Retention." *Technical & Skills Training,* January 1997, p. 4.

Thiagarajan, Sivasailam. "A Game for Cooperative Learning." *Training & Development,* May 1992, pp. 35-41.

West, Karen L. "Effective Training for a Revolving Door." *Training & Development,* September 1996, pp. 50-52.

Books

Baridon, Andrea, and David R. Eyler. *Sexual Harassment Awareness Training: 60 Practical Activities for Trainers.* New York: McGraw-Hill, 1996.

Boyan, Lee, and Rosalind Enright. *High-Performance Sales Training: 64 Interactive Projects.* New York: AMACOM, 1992.

Consalvo, Carmine M. *Outdoor Games for Trainers.* Brookfield, VT: Gower, 1995.

Eitington, Julius E. *The Winning Trainer.* Houston: Gulf Publishing, 1984.

Elgood, Chris. *Handbook of Management Games.* (5th edition). Aldershot, Hampshire, UK: Gower Press, 1993.

Engel, Herbert M. *Handbook of Creative Learning Exercises.* Amherst, MA: HRD Press, 1994.

Kirby, Andy. *Encyclopedia of Games for Trainers.* Amherst, MA: HRD Press, 1992.

Kirk, James J., and Lynne D. Kirk. *Training Games for Career Development.* New York: McGraw-Hill, 1995.

Newstrom, John W., and Edward E. Scannell. *Still More Games Trainers Play: Experiential Learning Exercises.* New York: McGraw-Hill, 1991.

Nilson, Carolyn D. *Games That Drive Change.* New York: McGraw-Hill, 1995.

———. *More Team Games for Trainers.* New York: McGraw-Hill, 1998.

———. *Team Games for Trainers.* New York: McGraw-Hill, 1993.

Scannell, Edward E., and John W. Newstrom. *Even More Games Trainers Play.* New York: McGraw-Hill, 1994.

———. *Games Trainers Play.* New York: McGraw-Hill, 1980.

Sikes, Sam. *Feeding the Zircon Gorilla.* Tulsa, OK: Learning Unlimited, 1995.

Thiagarajan, Sivasailam, and Raja Thiagarajan. *Each Teach: Harnessing the Power of Team Learning.* Amherst, MA: HRD Press, 1995.

———. *Interactive Lectures: Add Participation to Your Presentation.* Amherst, MA: HRD Press, 1995.

———. *Take Five: A Participatory Strategy for Better Brainstorming.* Amherst, MA: HRD Press, 1995.

Ukens, Lorraine L. *Getting Together: Icebreakers and Group Energizers.* San Francisco: Jossey-Bass, 1996.

———. *Working Together: 55 Team Games.* San Francisco: Jossey-Bass, 1996.

Infolines

Darraugh, Barbara (ed.). "More Great Games." No. 9106.

Preziosi, Robert. "Icebreakers: Warm Up Your Audience." No. 8911.

Job Aid

Game Selection Checklist

The appropriate game can make your presentation or training session one of the most memorable and productive experiences of your trainees' careers—but before you select a particular game, know the answers to the following questions:

☐ What is your purpose for using the game? What should it communicate to the group?

_____

_____

☐ What is the game's central focus? How does it serve your learning goals for the group?

_____

_____

☐ How large is your training group? What are their backgrounds? Are they familiar with the training material? With each other?

_____

_____

☐ Is the game adaptable to the needs of your training program? Can you use it to introduce, demonstrate, or reinforce the training?

_____

_____

☐ How "playable" is the game? Try it. How is it organized? Does it work according to its instructions? Is it fun?

_____

_____

☐ Do you have the resources and facilities for the game?

_____

_____

☐ Is this game the best way to achieve your objectives?

_____

_____

INFO LINE

PRESENTATION SKILLS & GAMES

Learn the secrets to becoming everyone's favorite speaker and make the entire process more fun and effective for everyone involved... including yourself. Even if you are a trainer or professional who uses presentations throughout the course of your career, you'll want these issues that teach you how to break the ice and gain interest, get lasting results from your presentations, overcome your fear of public speaking, and bring more excitement to your training programs.

10 Great Games And How to Use Them

Discover the learning value of games, exercises, and puzzles. Revised edition.

Print Product Code: 258411
PDF Product Code: 758411

How to Prepare and Use Effective Visual Aids

Learn the general principles of visual design and how they can guide your use of other visual aids. A sample presentation plan helps keep you on track. Revised edition.

Print Product Code: 258410
PDF Product Code: 758410

Effective Classroom Training Techniques

This *Infoline* is a primer on the use of the most effective techniques—including icebreakers, questioning, brainstorming, case studies, role playing, demonstrations, simulations, games, and more. The issue will show you how to develop these training techniques and offers advice for their appropriate use in the classroom.

Print Product Code: 250108
PDF Product Code: 750108

Ice Breakers

Provides an overview of different icebreakers: openers, acquainters, games, and brainstorming as well as guidelines for selecting icebreakers.

Print Product Code: 258911
PDF Product Code: 758911

Fun in the Workplace

Get the best from "Thiagi" with a training technique called interactive lectures (or lecture games) that combines elements from the lecture method and from training games. Contains detailed instructions for conducting six different lecture games.

Print Product Code: 250105
PDF Product Code: 750105

Improve Your Communication and Speaking Skills

This issue presents techniques for overcoming the fear of public speaking, using nonverbal cues, and avoiding presentation pitfalls. It includes a job aid which is a speaker's assessment instrument.

Print Product Code: 259409

ORDERING IS AS EASY AS:

1. Go to the ASTD online store at store.astd.org
2. Search for the *Infoline* single issue by the Print Product Order or PDF Product Code or
3. Call ASTD Customer Care at 800.628.2783

Infoline Pricing	Single Issue		12-Month Subscription	
	Print	PDF	US	INTL
ASTD Member	$10	$19.95	$99	$139
Nonmember	$12	$24.95	$139	$179

Download your **Infoline Catalog** today at infoline.astd.org!

PDFs only available for purchase at store.astd.org   Prices valid through December 2008. Subject to change thereafter.

08073662410

ASTD
WORKPLACE LEARNING & PERFORMANCE
PRESS

Printed in the United States
136948LV00003B